Big Animals

by Cara Torrance

OXFORD
UNIVERSITY PRESS
AUSTRALIA & NEW ZEALAND

Big Animals

Look at these animals. You will see that they all have one thing in common. They are very large.

Big animals live all around the world. They live on the land and in the sea.

The red kangaroo, brown bear, elephant and blue whale are some of the biggest animals on the planet. They share some features, while other features are more unusual.

The elephant is the only animal with such a long trunk.

Red Kangaroo

The red kangaroo is the largest animal in Australia. It is as tall as an average adult man and extremely heavy.

A baby red kangaroo is the size of a jelly bean when it is born.

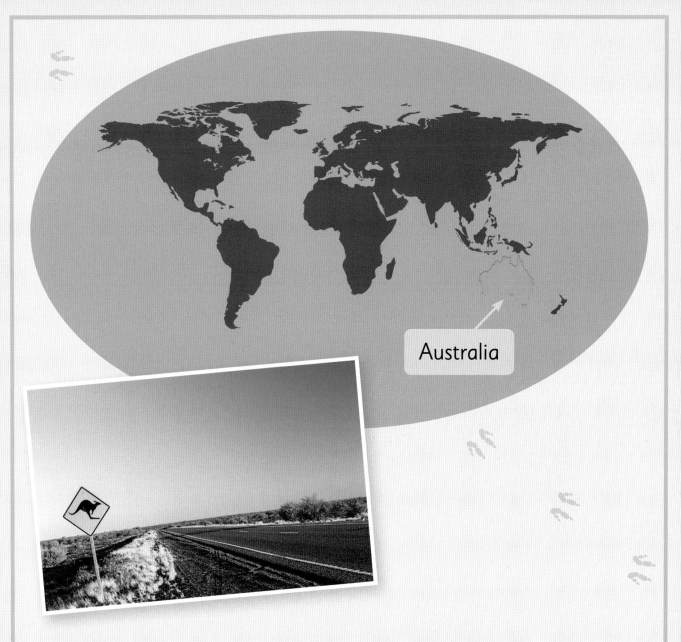

Australia

The red kangaroo is found only in Australia. It lives mostly in grassland and scrubland. It also lives in desert regions.

Features

The red kangaroo has long, muscular back legs and short front legs. It has a long, thick tail, pointy ears and a square **snout**. The female has a pouch on its front to protect its babies.

snout

pouch

Baby red kangaroos will stay in the pouch until they are eight months old.

The red kangaroo's tail helps it to balance. Sharp claws, especially the back claws, are a red kangaroo's fighting tool.

Interesting Fact !

Red kangaroos are tough kickboxers, using their powerful back legs to attack **opponents**.

Brown Bear

The brown bear is one of the two largest bears in the world. The other is the polar bear.

Both bears are much bigger than a human.

The brown bear is also known as the 'grizzly bear'.

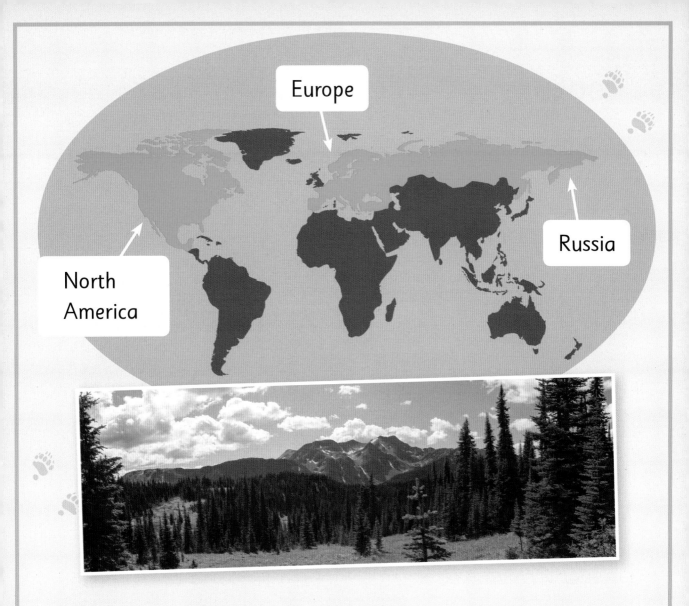

The brown bear is mostly found in Europe, North America and Russia. It tends to live in mountain woodlands and meadows but can also be found along coastlines.

Features

The brown bear has very strong **limbs**. It has huge front paws with large, sharp claws, and a long, straight snout.

hump

snout

sharp claws

An unusual feature of the brown bear is the hump of muscle above its shoulders.

The brown bear's strong legs help it to run faster than the world's fastest human athlete. The brown bear is a good digger and builder.

Interesting Fact !

The brown bear is extremely good at picking up a scent. Its sense of smell is around 100 times better than a human's.

The brown bear can run at up to 64 kilometres per hour.

African Bush Elephant

The African bush elephant is the biggest living land animal.

A baby bush elephant can be as heavy as a large human adult male.

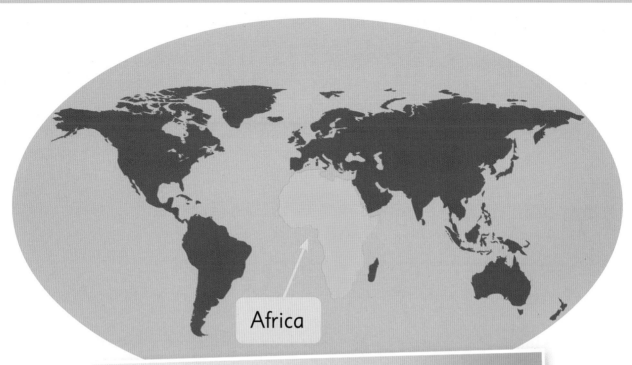

The African bush elephant is found in Africa where it moves through grasslands in a **clan**. There may be hundreds of elephants travelling in a clan.

Features

The African bush elephant is tall with long, strong legs. The most unusual feature of the African bush elephant is its long trunk.

large ears

long tusks

strong legs

long trunk

The African bush elephant's huge ears allow it to release heat. It uses its tusks to feed, dig and fight.

Elephants use their trunk to do many things. They use it to pick up and hold things, push, reach up high and suck up water.

Interesting Fact !

The biggest known elephant weighed almost 11 000 kilograms. This is more than the weight of 120 heavy adult men.

Blue Whale

The blue whale is the biggest living animal on the planet.

Blue whale babies are the biggest babies in the world. They are 500 times bigger than human babies.

Adult blue whales are about the length of three buses.

blue whale **habitat**

Blue whales are found around the world and
move to different places depending on the season.
People rarely see them as they spend a lot of
time underwater.

Features

The blue whale has a huge flat head and a large mouth. It has a special filter-feeding system, known as baleen. A blue whale opens its mouth and takes in lots of fish and water. The baleen keeps the fish inside the whale to eat and lets the water back out.

flat head

baleen

The blue whale eats huge amounts at a time. This food is stored as fat in its large body. It may be months before the whale eats again.

Interesting Fact

The blue whale's heart is about the size of a car.

About Big Animals

Big animals are amazing!

How big?

The blue whale is too big for the page!

blue whale

African bush elephant

brown bear

red kangaroo

How heavy?

Animal	Weight
Blue whale	up to 173 000 kilograms
Elephant	up to 10 600 kilograms
Brown bear	up to 390 kilograms
Red kangaroo	up to 91 kilograms

Glossary

clan: a group of elephants moving together

habitat: the place where an animal lives

limbs: arms, legs or wings

opponents: those you compete against in a fight

snout: the front part of an animal's head, with its nose and mouth

tusks: a pair of long, curved, pointy teeth

Index